Women Overcoming Weight Loss

12 Step Program for Manual for Women

T.R.A.C Publishing
P.O. Box 1243
Austell, GA 30168

ISBN-13: 978-0692255384
ISBN-10: 0692255389

For inquiries contact Shakisha Edness
770-369-4681

TABLE OF CONTENTS

INTRODUCTION

This workbook is designed to help women lose weight emotionally, mentally, and physically. It will help them shed unwanted pounds (weight gain) in every area. Everyone wants to lose weight, but cannot afford to hire a therapist and/or personal trainer. So I created this book to help you do it yourself, along with God.

This book will strengthen you spiritually and financially because when you think high thoughts, it shapes you to become higher in every area of your life. You will get your emotions under control and learn to control them; not allowing them to control you or make you lose control.

Your thoughts are ultimately the breeding ground for everything that you say and do. Also, the way you view yourself and others; the way you respond to others and allow others to respond to you. Know what to take in and to keep out.

I am not focusing on where you have been; but where you are, where you are going, and the information and directions to get you there. Along with focusing on who you are and how to totally embrace yourself.

How you got there seriously is not my question, because it was either by being misled, forced, or by choice.

But once you got there, you realized you should not be there. Now the question is... how do I get out of here?

We cannot do anything about our past but to acknowledge it, accept it, and appreciate it!

The one thing we all have in common, is that we purchased this book because we want to lose weight.

INTERVIEW

Interview:
A meeting in which one person elicits information from another.

Inter:
To bury or entomb.

Entomb:
To bury or trap in or under something.

Inter – View

Have you had to prepare for an interview? Can you remember faxing or emailing the potential future employer your well groomed resume' and receiving a phone call asking if you were available for an interview? Were you excited? I know I was. Then, immediately after hanging up, you began trying to figure out what will I wear. Not to mention your hair, nails, shoes, accessories, and make – up. Because you wanted to make a great impression on the interviewer, so you could get the job.

The big day came; you couldn't sleep all night because you were anxious to get this interview over with. You have already anticipated that you are getting this job. You have named it, claimed it, believed it, and you received it, In Jesus' Name Amen!

You looked amazing. You couldn't stop looking in the mirror as you drove to the job interview. Your hair was flawless, your nails and toes matched. Your lipstick was topnotch and the outfit was stunning.

As you parked the car you began to pray, "God your will, have your way. Please God let me get this job."

Immediately, you began to look at the resume' and lifting it up to Jesus, because you know more than half of it is false information. You went over all the information on it, trying to memorize it. You do not only know its false information on it, you know the truth! You are praying to God, "Please forgive me but you know I need this job."

Take a glance at the above definitions one more time.

Now let me explain what is about to take place. You have just arrived to your interview. Welcome!

A meeting has been scheduled for you to elicit information from yourself, about yourself. The information is that of which you have buried. The only person who knows the place of burial is you, and you have frequent visits there. You visit the burial site whenever someone angers you, hurts you, or sometimes when you are alone with yourself.

This interview is much different from the ones you have prepared for because, you're the interviewer. It is about the "inter – you". So no need to impress anyone else, just express you!

Let me be clearer. The workbook you are holding has an exterior (which is the cover), and it also has an interior (which is the content that you are reading now). The exterior is just a picture but the interior tells the truth.

Let's define interior.
Interior: The inside.

Now let's define view.
View: The act of seeing or examining; range of vision; something seen, one's opinion or belief. To look at, to examine; to consider; to regard in a certain way.

Thank you so much for being brave enough to go under the magnifying glass. Allowing your flaws to be seen, treated, healed, delivered, and restored.

This interview is not about playing dress up or impressing anyone. It is about keeping it real with you. If you cannot be real with yourself, you cannot be real or keep it real with anyone else.

I am grateful that you are going down the journey of getting to know yourself, liking yourself, loving yourself, appreciating yourself, and most of all being yourself without anyone's permission.

This is a remedy of assistance to improve you. Everyone can always use a little home improvement.

This manual won't only set you free, but it will direct you to your true purpose in life. So get on your mark, get set, and go.

God, thank you for allowing this information to help, the woman holding this book, to assist in answering every question to the best of her ability. In her own timing, I ask you to guide her during this process which will overall help her progress in her future.

May His Mercy, Grace, and Favor rest upon your life.   In Jesus' Name, Amen.

The interviewing process begins.

Name: _____

Date: _____

Age: _____

Address: _____

City and State: _____

Weigh yourself: _____

Measurements

Neck: _____

Breast: _____

Waist: _____

Butt: _____

Arms: _____

Ankles: _____

Thighs: _____

Legs: _____

Above breast: _____

Below breast: _____

Why do you want to lose weight?

_____

_____

_____

_____

_____

If given the tools to lose weight, will you put forth an effort to lose weight?

_____

This is not a diet!
This is a new way of living and eating healthy!

Your coach is just a click away.

Life Coach Shakisha Edness @ www.womenovercoming.com

MIRROR THERAPY

Mirror:
A surface that reflects a visual image.

Therapy:
A type of treatment.

Treatment:
The act, manner, or process of dealing with something, a measure or measures designed to heal or alleviate.

Let's identify the illness that needs treatment. So many people want others to change their behavior, attitude, actions, and reactions. But if they are not aware of what to change, how can they change? This is when we should take a look in the mirror and do a self - evaluation, enabling us to identify with whatever is crippling our growth. Therefore, this enables us to love ourselves right where we are, for who we are. The mistakes we've made do not define who we are!

When was the last time you looked in the mirror?

_____

_____

_____

_____

_____

Do you avoid looking in the mirror? If so, why?

_____

_____

_____

_____

Today we will face ourselves, by facing the mirror.

In order to acknowledge it, we must identify it.

Let's define acknowledge.

Acknowledge: To admit or confess; to certify, as valid; to show appreciation; to confirm receipt of.

Acknowledge is to recognize, admit, and confess.

In order to acknowledge where you are, let me introduce you to mirror therapy.

Mirror therapy is to help you identify with and connect with yourself right where you are.

Please get a camera, ask someone to take a picture of you, develop it, and place it here. Make sure it is a full body picture.

Mirror Therapy

1. What do you see when you look at yourself?

   _____

   _____

   _____

2. Who do you see when you look at yourself?

   _____

   _____

   _____

3. How do you feel about what/who you see?

   _____

   _____

   _____

4. How do you feel about yourself?

   _____

   _____

   _____

5. Where do you see yourself right now?

   _____

   _____

   _____

   Name five top qualities you like about yourself?

1. _____

2. _____

3. _____

4. _____

5. _____

Name five things you wish to change about yourself.

1. _____

2. _____

3. _____

4. _____

5. _____

Why do you want to change the things listed above?

_____

_____

_____

Can you change them? If not, can you accept it and learn how to embrace it?

_____

_____

_____

What do you display to others about yourself?

_____

_____

_____

What defines you?

_____

_____

_____

What do you believe about yourself?

_____

_____

_____

1. Do you have a plan for your life? _____
2. What is your plan for your life? _____
3. Does your plan accommodate you? _____
4. Does your plan accommodate others? _____

Name three to five things (morally) you live by regardless.
1. _____
2. _____
3. _____
4. _____
5. _____

As we know, people play important roles in our lives. So the following questions are about you and others.

Let's call this the rearview mirror of mirror therapy.

Who do you admire? Why?

_____

_____

_____

Who challenges the best in you to become better?

_____

_____

_____

Who assists you in being stagnant? Keeps you stuck.

_____

_____

_____

Who provokes you to do well?

_____

_____

_____

Who provokes you to do poorly?

_____

_____

_____

Who helps you to prosper?

_____

_____

_____

Who are you comfortable with?

_____

_____

_____

Who are you uncomfortable with?

_____

_____

_____

Who do you feel safe with? Are you safe with them? Just because we feel safe with someone, doesn't mean we are really safe with them.

_____

_____

_____

_____

Who intimidates you? Why? How?

_____

_____

_____

_____

Back to YOU again.

1. Are you comfortable being yourself? _____
2. Are you comfortable being alone with yourself? _____
3. Who do you want to become? _____
4. Who are you now? _____
5. Who are you? _____

Everything happens in an atmosphere.

Where are you now?

_____

_____

_____

Where do you want to be?

_____

_____

_____

Where do you see yourself in the future?

_____

_____

_____

Where do you feel safe? Are you safe there? Just because you feel safe there, does not mean you are safe there.

_____

_____

_____

Where do you feel uncomfortable?

_____

_____

_____

_____

Where do you feel comfortable?

_____

_____

_____

Where do you feel unsafe?

_____

_____

_____

Where do you feel you are able to be yourself?

_____

_____

_____

Does you environment compliment you?   If so, how?

_____

_____

_____

Execute the plan.

1. How do you plan to become who you want to be? _____

2. How do you plan to get to where you want to be? _____

3. How can you do what you desire to do? _____

4. How do you know it will work? _____

5. How do you know it won't work? _____

6. How many times will you try before giving up? _____

Nothing beats a failure but a try, so giving up should never be an option.

1. What are your thoughts toward yourself?

_____

_____

_____

_____

_____

2. Are they good?

_____

3. Are they bad?

_____

4. Are they true?

_____

Bonus question:
Are the true things about you <u>the truth</u>?

_____

Example:
It's true that you are 100lbs over weight, but that can be changed, so it's not the truth forever. It's true for today.

Therapy: A type of treatment.
Regardless if this is being done in a group setting or alone, it is still individual therapy.

If you were sick and someone had the antidote to cure you, will you reject it or accept it?

I am not a doctor nor am I a therapist, but I have been through some things and I went to therapy.

My therapist did one thing or shall I say two. She asked questions and allowed me to answer them. What began taking place was that the questions stirred up emotions and I started asking myself questions. Then, I began getting important answers to the questions asked.

Finally, I had a "wow" and "aha" experience; as Oprah will say!

Saying to myself, "That's why I act this way, respond that way, and perceive things the way that I do."

But if my therapist never asked the important questions and allowed me to answer them, my perception and my life would still be in the same place.

I've learned to become my own therapist, but God is my psychologist!

Therapist:
A person skilled in a particular kind of therapy.

Psychologist:
Touching on the mind or emotions.

Psychotherapist:
Treatment for a mental or emotional disorder.
If I need medication, Jesus is all the medicine I need.

ACCEPTANCE

Acceptance:
To embrace as truth. To agree or approve. To receive or take what is offered.

I accept who I am. But I am striving to become more comfortable with allowing me be myself with everyone, in all my surroundings.

Answer the following acceptance questions below.

What do others say about you? _____
Managers or supervisors? _____
Mate/Spouse? _____
Coworkers? _____
Best friend? _____
Worst friend? _____
Mother? _____
Father? _____
Siblings? _____
Children? _____

Is it true? _____
Do you agree? _____
Do you accept it? _____

Let's flip the coin.

What do you say about them? _____
Is it true or truth? _____

Your truth does not have to be true to others. And others' truth does not have to be true to you. Its two sides to a story, and only one truth!

Though it's true today that you have a nasty attitude, does not mean it's a truth. Never say, "Well this is how I am." Remember you can change.

We do not necessarily change who we are. But we change what we do, which in return helps make us better. And eventually promotes us to become our best.

Many focus on being the best, meaning better than everyone else, rather than becoming their best.

Every person's opinion about you came from an action you displayed before them. Put your best behavior on display, at all times. Others are taking inventory of you.

Continuation of acceptance questions...

Do you accept the following?

Who you are? _____

What you've done? _____

Where you've been? _____

If so, explain:

_____

_____

_____

_____

_____

If not, explain:

_____

_____

_____

_____

_____

Do you accept why you did it? _____

Who you did it with? _____

Were you vulnerable, insecure, or coerced? _____

Did you learn from it? _____

What did you learn from it?

_____

_____

_____

_____

In your own words, write down what you accept about your past?

_____

_____

_____

_____

_____

_____

_____

Acceptance is the key to moving forward.
You are not what happened to you.
You are not what you did.
You are not what happened around you.

Acceptance helps you to forgive.
I forgive them and myself.

Acceptance helps you get to a place of appreciation.
I accept what I did, how I did it, why I did it, when and where I did it, and who I did it with.
Because nothing I did affected who I am.

NOTES

SERENITY PRAYER

God grant me the **Serenity** to accept the things I cannot change... **Courage** to change the things I can and **Wisdom** to know the difference...

Grant is to give.

Serenity is to be untroubled. To be tranquil.

Accepatance is to agree or take what's offered.
(The things I cannot change).

Courage is the quality that allows others to face danger or adversity with confidence.
(To change the things I can).

Wisdom is the ability to make sound judgment.
(To know the difference between what I can/cannot change).

This is where women have to understand that they are powerless over people, places, and things. They only have the power to change their own lives no, but one else's. This has been taught in various NA/AA meetings. It has helped many across the nation and it's helpful to all that applies it.

It's amazing because we're asking God to give us an untroubled spirit, to accept what we cannot change, but the confidence to change what we can. If we can change it, why do we need confidence?

We still need God to help us, because one of the hardest things is changing yourself. That's the only person you can change.

Trying to change others is nonsense. That's why we need wisdom, in order to know the difference between the two. (To make a sound judgment to differentiate between the two).

I really hope you are understanding this, because once you get this nothing can stop you.

EXPOSURE

Exposure:
Is to lay open, reveal, or leave unprotected.

Women have been taught that what goes on in their house, stays in their house. This has created them to hide from themselves, holding in what has happened to them. Things such as: molestation, abandonment, rape (that has brought on insecurities), shame, doubt, fear, hopelessness, poverty way of thinking, depression, and even isolation. We create the atmosphere for them to feel comfortable to expose anything and everything. So they may become free of the hurt and pain.

Do you remember hearing your mother saying, "What goes on in my house, stays in my house"? And my mother wasn't playing about that above statement and I am sure yours wasn't either.

The secrets that are not exposed causes illnesses, and God cannot heal that of which you won't expose.

An uncured illness, is like cancer in its fourth dimension.

Do not be afraid of uncovering what you've done or what has been done to you. Because the best feeling of being exposed, is taking the covers off of yourself.

Let's get naked!

What happened to you?

_____

_____

_____

_____

Who did it to you?

_____

_____

_____

_____

Did they violate or abandon you?

_____

_____

_____

_____

Did it cause you to isolate yourself or mistrust? Did their spirit transfer into you causing you to do to others what was done to you?

_____

_____

_____

_____

When did this happen to you?

_____

Where did it happen to you?

_____

Why do you think it happened? Do you think it could have been avoided? If so, how?

_____

_____

_____

_____

_____

Who do you feel is responsible for this being able to happen to you?

_____

Why were they responsible?

_____

_____

Have you discussed this matter with your offender? If so, what was their response?

_____

_____

_____

_____

_____

If not, why not? Are you afraid, angry, hurt, or embarrassed? What emotions do you have attached to this situation?

Have you told anyone other than your offender about it?

_____

Did they suggest you get over it? Have you gotten over it or have you buried it?

_____

_____

In order to get over it, you must uncover it. Yes, dig it up and expose it.
To expose is to report the facts about something.

You have held this secret for such a long time and it has done major damage to you, other relationships, and potentially can destroy any future relationships. It is time for you to set it free so you yourself can be freed.

The facts are that it happened and someone caused it to happen. Someone failed at protecting you or no one had any way of protecting you from it. It could have been that you trusted someone, but they took advantage of you. Molesting someone's innocence, doesn't necessarily mean physically. It can be emotionally and mentally. But what happened affected you and your life emotionally, mentally, physically, socially, and spiritually. In some instances, financially. And it's time to stop protecting that of which was designed to destroy you.

FORGIVENESS

Forgiveness:
To pardon/overlook.

The simplicity of things always seem to work, not making things so complicated. The strategy used here has been phenomenal. Hatred doesn't hurt the hated, it hurts the hater! To forgive is to have control over your life and not allow someone else to control you. We present this simply as to overlook their offense. A lot of people become bitter, which the bitterness works more internally and becomes sickness in their body.

This is where women learn to ask for forgiveness and make amends. Forgive others and their offense. Because though you forgive the person, the offense can come up again through another. So we teach to forgive both the offense and the offender, so you will be immune to it. It's most important to forgive yourself for the past mistakes and poor judgments.

Peel to heal.
Peel: To come off or strip off.
Exfoliate hurt, resentment, jealously, bitterness, hate, insecurities, shame, guilt, and/or anger.

Exfoliate: To peel off, to remove or come off, layers.

To forgive self and others, is to set free and become free.

F – Forgive.
R – Redeemed.
E – Elevate.
E – Evolve and Enjoy…

I can… I will…
Forgive myself, others, and their offenses.
So I can peel to heal.

Part I. Forgiveness toward others.
Ask yourself the following questions.

1. Who do I hold resentment against? _____

2. Why do I hold resentment against them? _____

3. Did they hurt me intentionally? _____

4. Are they aware that they hurt me? _____

5. Have I told them what they did to me? _____

6. Have I expressed how it affected me, our relationship, and my relationship with others?
    _____

7. How long have I held this against them? _____

8. How long have I hurt? _____

9. When was the last time I spoke with them? _____

10. When I see them; how do I feel? _____

11. When seeing them, do I get angry all over again? _____

12. Do my anxieties take over? _____

13. Do I not trust others, due to this event taking place in my life? _____

14. Where did it happen? _____

15. When I visit the place, does it bring back memories? Are they painful? _____

16. Do I talk about it to myself or others? _____

17. What suggestions do others give to me? Is it good or bad advice? _____

18. Do I love the person that hurt me? _____

19. Do I like or dislike them? _____

20. Do I dislike their ways? _____

21. Do I want to befriend them again? Why? Why not?

_____

_____

_____

22. Do I believe in restoration? _____

RESTORATION
Do you believe God can restore people and relationships? _____

Is this relationship worth restoring? _____

Is the person worth being restored? _____

Are you worth being restored? _____

Open your heart to forgive who did it.
Write them a letter, explaining what they did and how it affected you. Also, explain why you are writing them, who they did it to, and what you want to come out of this.

"Regardless, I forgive you and me. Thank you because I am a better person with a better understanding."

Love Ms. Forgiveness, Forgetful, and Over-looker.

There are three important letters that must be written from you. One letter to the person that offended you, the other letter to yourself, and then a letter to God.

Yes, they did it (I don't deny that), but I forgive my offender and their offense.

Matthew 18: 15
"If another believer sins against you, go privately and point out the fault. If the person listens and confesses it, you have won that person back."

Part II. Forgiveness toward yourself.
The worst pain is the pain one inflicts on themselves.

1. What did I do? _____

2. Why did I do it? Was it intentional? _____

3. Who did I do it with or against? _____

4. Did I hurt others in the process of doing it? _____

5. Where did I do it? _____

6. How did I do it? _____

7. When did I do it? _____

8. Am I ashamed of it? _____

9. Am I ashamed of myself? _____

10. Will I do it again? _____

11. How do I know I won't do it again? Will? _____

12. Why do I believe I won't? _____

13. Why do I believe you will? _____

14. Who did I see do this first? Last? _____

15. Am I what I did? _____

16. Was it fun? _____

17. Did it hurt? _____

18. Does it still hurt? _____

19. Are you what you did? No. Forgive yourself!

20. Did I make amends to those that I hurt, by asking for forgiveness? _____

Make a sincere apology and appreciate the forgiveness of another. But forgive self!

I cannot unlock the door to forgiveness, if you won't give me the key. Though you have the key, if not used, what's the use?

Admit it! Quit it! Repent of it! Forget it!

Yes, I did it. No, I will not do it anymore. I've asked for forgiveness. I forgave myself.
It's behind me. Now I must move on.

Philippians 3: 13.
No, dear brothers and sisters, I am still not all I should be, but I am focusing all my energies on this one thing: Forgetting the past and looking forward to what lies ahead.

Part III. Forgiveness from God.

1. Did I do something to offend God? _____

2. What did I do? _____

3. Why did I do it? _____

4. Who did I do it with? _____

5. Where was the sin committed? _____

6. Am I embarrassed? _____

7. Did I enjoy doing it? _____

8. How did I feel afterwards? _____

9. What did I do afterwards? Did I stop attending church services? _____

10. Do you feel like a hypocrite? _____

11. Have you talked to God about it? _____

12. Have you asked for forgiveness? _____

13. Do you believe you are forgiven? _____

14. Have you did it again? If so, why? If not, why not? _____

15. Do you feel you let God down? _____

16. Do you have the strength to get up again? _____

17. Do you know God forgives? _____

18. Do you accept His forgiveness? _____

I admit my sin. I repent of my sin. I ask for forgiveness. God has forgiven me. I know I am forgiven. I am free to start over.

Micah 7: 19
Once again you will have compassion on us. You will trample our sins under your feet and throw them into the depths of the ocean.

Let me give you a helping hand.

     I.   Get up.
     II. Go to God.
     III. Talk with God.
     IV. Admit your sin.
     V. Repent of your sins.
     VI. Pray and ask for forgiveness.
     VII.   Listen to God.
     VIII.   Go and sin no more.

He cleanses, delivers, and sets you free.

NOTES

DELIVERANCE

Deliverance:
The condition of being set free. Having the ability to perform well.

Perform:
To act on and complete, to function; to present in public for entertainment.

You must deliver your cares, so He can deliver you!

Women must be aware that their freedom is a direct connection to their overall performance. In order to perform well, you must be freed; mentally, emotionally, physically, and spiritually. Any restraint hinders their capability to achieve.

Performance questions.

1. Do you perform well? _____

2. Do you finish what you start? _____

3. Do you give yourself reasons for not finishing? (Excuses.)_____

4. Whose fault is it, if you have incomplete tasks? _____

5. Do you rush to get finish just to say it's done? _____

6. Do you take your time to make sure it's done well? _____

7. Do you recheck your work after it's completed? Why? Why not? _____

8. If you notice you forgot something, will your correct it or just let it pass (as if you didn't notice)? _____

9. Do you prepare your day ahead of schedule or do you just go with the flow? _____

10. Do you set goals? If so, how often… daily, weekly, monthly, or yearly? _____

11. Are you early, on time, or late? (You are aware that being on time is late) _____

12. Do you look forward to tomorrow or dread that it is coming? _____

13. Do you look for every performance opportunity? _____

14. Do you complain when it's an opportunity to perform? _____

15. Can you multi task? _____

16. Are you willing to do janitorial duties as a receptionist? _____

17. Do you only do what your job description defines? _____

18. Can you arrive earlier than your scheduled time? _____

19. Can you stay later than you're scheduled to get off? _____

20. Do you think before responding? _____

21. Are your giving your best performance or just enough to get by? _____

Imagine yourself being an actor and you are the main character in the play. Thousands of people paid to come see you perform. How would you want to be remembered? What will you want their reactions to be? Would you want them to attend more plays you're starring in? Would you want them to tell others about the play?

We have the opportunity everyday (while at home, work, church, and in public places) to perform well. Majority of us do not have a clue. And many wonder why others won't support them. That's why! Because people seen your overall performance with others, while at work, home, church, and in the public; they are not pleased.

They've heard the lies you told to others about others. They've witnessed you doing things that were wrong. But you gave yourself the excuse that no one is watching or that everyone does it. They saw you leave for lunch, but not clocking out implying you worked all the way through. They know you blamed your coworker for not telling you about the new software, but they know that they did. They saw you intentionally hang up on the customer and then logging off the phone, claiming it to be a dropped call.

People see others perform every day and they refuse to invest in that type of business. So instead of it being sold out, it's canceled!

Though we can be the main character of the play. There are still important roles of others such as the director, manager, supervisor, and coworkers.

1. What do those that work with you (from day to day) say about your overall performance? _____

2. Would they say you are a team player?

   _____

3. Would they say you are punctual?

   _____

4. Would they say it's a pleasure to work with you?

   _____

5. Have they said how much they appreciate you?

   _____

6. How will they describe your attitude?

   _____

Remember if there is a duplication of one thing being said about you, by several different people, it might need your attention to find out if it's true.

If you're having technical difficulties performing well, ask yourself if you operate in the following list below.

Some people struggle with the various issues and it hinders their performance.

- Controlling spirit.
- Manipulative spirit.
- Spirit of deception.
- Jealousy spirit.
- Complaining spirit.
- Lazy spirit.
- Gossiping spirit.
- Procrastinating spirit.

And the list goes on. We must be delivered and set free, so we can perform at our best.

Everyone knows what's wrong with them, because someone has pointed it out. But we sometimes refuse to take criticism of any kind, even constructive criticism is not appreciated anymore.

But remember I said that I am not worried about where you've been or how you got there. I am concerned about where you are, where you're going, and helping you get there safely.

If you need to be delivered from anything, the first thing is to acknowledge what it is that has you in bondage. Acknowledge who has you entangled and admit that you are stuck. Then, decide that you want to be free.

You freedom depends upon you making a decision to become free!

It's much like an addict. They must recognize they have a problem with drugs, admit they are an addict, and decide they do not want to continue to be a slave to it. Seek help to stop!

This can be an addiction to drugs, alcohol, sex, the need to be needed, etc.

If you are in need of being delivered and you want to be free, do the following:

Get alone with God, cry out to Him, Acknowledge your problem, admit it to Him, and Ask for His assistance for deliverance. Thank Him in advance, because help is on the way.

After you rise up, change your old habits by replacing them with new habits. Change bad habits into good habits. Some habits are not bad, but they are old and no longer work. Others are bad and they must be replaced with the new.

Learn to accommodate the following:
Think things through before giving a response, verbally or physically.
Plan ahead of time.
Set short term, long term, and immediate goals.
Write your plan out step by step.
Play scratch off, by scratching off the assignment as you finish it.
Always know where you are going and the route to get you there.
Make a U-turn or take a detour when road work is ahead.
Look forward to the next day; the next assignment lives there.
Ask for help and lend a helping hand.
Do it while their eyes are on you and when their backs are turned.
Practice saying, "Thank you. You are Welcome. I Apologize."

HEALING

Healing:
The process of making or becoming sound or healthy again.

Become:
To change into or to grow into being.

Make:
To bring into existence by shaping.

Women Overcoming Weight Loss is overall designed to create the atmosphere and provide the tools to help women make the necessary changes for them to become healthy.

When reading anything, depending on the words that you put the emphasis on determines what understanding or knowledge you will receive.

The topic of this chapter is healing. But the focus word or the word that I am applying the emphasis, is PROCESS.

It clearly states that healing is the process of making or becoming sound or healthy again.

Let's define process.

Process is a set of actions; a system.

Actions is putting forth, or exerting energy; decisiveness. The result of activity; a manner of movement. Parts that move in a mechanism. A thing done. One's behavior or conduct.

Are you getting through this process?
Come on… don't give up now.

Movement is a change of position, a steady or gradual change.
To move is to be active.

Mechanism is action.

Pursuit is to hunt or chase, an activity.

Transaction is to accomplish.
Act is to perform.

Once you get through the process, it becomes a thing done. Meaning it is completed.

My God! I hope this exercise is speaking to you the way it is to me. In other words, you must do something to be healed!

Jesus died, so that He would Rise!
He did something!

The word says that by His stripes, we are healed. I hear people quote that scripture a lot when dealing with healing.

I am not saying it is not true. I am saying He was beaten, so he endured the pain. He did something to complete something!

I showed you the process by defining the words and it led us to something being done. Completed.

I must not end here though.

I have a few more words to define to bring this chapter to completion.

Let's define lively. Lively is marked by energy and spirit, active.
Lively is to be active, animated, brisk, energetic, spirited, and vivacious.

Woman of God, BUST A MOVE!

It is time for you to become active in an activity that will spring forth lively energy and bring life to your spirit, in Jesus' Name.

So if you need a healing spiritually, emotionally, mentally, socially, or financially; answer the following questions pertaining to it.

Spiritual Healing Questionnaire

If you need a financial increase (healing), what are you doing to get it?

- Do you know God or know of Him?
- Do you have a personal relationship with Him?
- Do you communicate with Him? If so, how often?
- Do you pray? If so, how often?
- Do you praise and worship God, in spirit and in truth?
- Do you own a bible?
- Do you read your bible?
- Do you understand what you read?
- Do you retain the information?
- Do you apply the information to your everyday life?
- Do you obey God?
- Do you obey His word?
- Do you fellowship with others about God?
- Do you attend a local church? Are you a member?
- Are you active in church?
- Do you use the gifts that God gave you, in the church?

Do you? Do you? Do you?
YOU MUST DO SOMETHING!

My spiritual healing depends on me doing something, so I commit myself to doing the following:

_____

_____

_____

_____

_____

_____

_____

_____

_____

_____

_____

_____

_____

Financial Healing Questionnaire

Have you cried out to God for a financial healing? Are you still crying? Okay wipe your tears away and answer the questions below.

- Are you financially stable?
- Do you work? Are you employed or self-employed?
- Do you not make enough, just enough, barely enough, enough, or more than enough?
- Do you work overtime?
- Are you working one or two jobs?
- What do you do with your "more than enough"?
- Do you live below, on, or above your level?
- Do you know where your money goes? If so, where? If not, look at your bank statement and receipts to track your money.

- Is it going in the right or wrong place?
- Do you tithe? If so, sometimes or all of the time? Before or after you pay your bills?
- If you do not tithe, why not? Do you feel you do not have enough to do so?
- Do you have a gift that is lying dormant, that can bring you a financial increase?
- If so, why are you not using it?
- Do you borrow money? If so, do you pay it back?

Do you? Do you? Do you?
YOU MUST DO SOMETHING!
My financial healing depends on me doing something, so I commit to doing the following:

_____
_____
_____
_____
_____
_____
_____
_____
_____
_____
_____
_____
_____
_____

Emotional Healing Questionnaire

- Are you an emotional wreck?
- Are you emotionally "wreck less"?
- How many wrecks are you having emotionally?

- How many emotional wrecks have you caused?

STOP!

If you were driving a car, and it got out of control. You hit a couple of mailboxes and was about to hit an individual; what will you do?

STOP THE CAR!

Learn how to **STOP** the emotional vehicle! It is wrecking your life, the lives of others, and relationships.

S – Sit down.
T – Think it through.
O – Observe your thoughts.
P – Pace your thoughts.

I am in control of the vehicle. I pay attention and obey all traffic laws. The signs are there to tell us when to slow down, proceed with caution, or to make an abrupt stop!

My emotional healing depends on me doing something, so I commit to doing the following:

_____

_____

_____

_____

_____

_____

_____

_____

_____

_____

_____

_____

Mental Healing Questionnaire

Have you ever had a thought and instantly you said, "No, I am not going to think like that"?

That's a clear sign, that mental healing is lightly knocking at the door.

Have you ever wished you hadn't said something immediately after saying it? That's another sign of mental healing knocking a little harder!

What about when you think about something, you begin speaking it out loud, and as you're speaking your body is going in the direction of your thoughts? And the entire time you are saying inside," Turn around; don't do it!"

The mental healing police is banging at the door, like the "Po Po's"!

Have you ever had the police to bang on your door, you got quiet, and ignored them?

That's exactly what you do when your thoughts are trying to protect you from yourself. Your mind is crying out for healing, but you're refusing to do what it is requesting of you.

The mental healing police is there to serve you a notice, saying that it is time to heal your thoughts.

Pay attention to the warning signs, because after they serve you they will subpoena you and arrest you soon after.

Let's get this thing thrown out by casting it out! In Jesus' Name.

Just because you think it does not mean it's true.

Your thoughts fertilize your feelings and actions.

My mental healing depends on me doing something, so I commit to do the following:

_____

_____

_____

_____

_____

_____

_____

Social Healing Questionnaire

- Are you in isolation?
- Do you associate with others?
- Do you speak to your neighbors, coworkers, or strangers?
- Do you speak first or must they speak to you first?
- Do you speak only if you're having a great day?
- Are you sarcastic when communicating with others?

- Are you direct when communicating with others?
- Are you opinionated when communicating with others?
- Do you feel your opinion means anything or everything?
- Do you allow others to communicate with you, without cutting them off?

This is where the healing takes place socially. Imagine yourself being taught how to drive a car. The main thing you're taught is to NOT just drive for yourself; but to drive for others. So make that above statement the golden rule here.

When communicating you're not just speaking for yourself, you are speaking to others.

Sometimes others will be wreck less, but you must pay attention so they don't hit you. They may run the stop sign and the red lights. But you STOP, let them go by, and do not cause a scene. Just throw up the yellow towel by saying that it is okay.

If they are wreck less with their words or going a thousand miles per hour, with you not being able to get a word in; this is a clear sign that they need to be heard.

A conversation is made up of the following:
Listening to others
Speaking to others
Understanding others
Knowing what to say, when to say it, or not to say anything at all!

My social healing depends on me doing something, so I commit to doing the following:

_____

_____

_____

_____

_____

_____

Physical Healing Questionnaire

Physical healing is everything above that has been shared but putting it into *ACTION*!

MOVEMENT shows there's still life. Anything that stays still will become dead.

When your feet stay still without the proper blood flow, they go to sleep. You must get up, stand on it, and move your toes so the blood can begin to flow appropriately… Amen.

You need a physical healing; get physical today!

- What is stopping you from getting up?
- Who is stopping you from getting up?
- Why are you being stopped?
- Where are you sitting?
- Who are you sitting with?
- What if it they or it never shows up?

- What are you waiting for?
- Who are you waiting on?
- Have they showed up yet?
- How long have you been waiting?
- Will you continue to miss your healing, because you are waiting on or for something?

The wait is waiting on you!

My physical healing depends on me doing something, so I commit to doing the following:

_____

_____

_____

_____

_____

_____

_____

_____

_____

_____

_____

_____

_____

RESTORATIVE MENTALITY

Restorative:
Having the power to restore. .

Mentality:
One's intellectual capacity; a manner of thinking.

The power to restoring your mentality is thinking positive thoughts about yourself and others, regardless of the circumstances and situations. We control our thoughts; they do not control us.

Proverbs 23:7
For as a man thinketh in his heart, so is he.

What are your thoughts toward yourself, your situations, others, and food?

_____

_____

Are they good, bad, or indifferent?

_____

_____

Are they true thoughts?

_____

_____

Are the true things about you today, the truth?

_____

_____

Ex: Do you ever have crazy thoughts that run through your mind? After having the thought, do you act upon it as if it was true?

_____

_____

True: Real, honest.

_____

Only to find out that it's not. What do you do when you find out it's not true?

_____

_____

Do you apologize afterwards? Or do you say, "Oh well"?

_____

_____

Truth: Fact.

Let's fast from negative thinking.
When you get a negative thought; immediately find a positive thought to replace it with.

Where your mind goes, your actions follows. Put your thoughts in the right place, so you will end up in the right place.

HEALTH & NUTRITION

Health:
Soundness of body or mind.

Nutrition:
The study of food and nourishment.

Soundness:
Healthy free from flaw or decay.

Nourish:
To provide the necessities for life and growth.

Good health is essential to become whole within your mind, body, and soul. We must eat well-balanced meals in order to live well-balanced lives. There is a saying, "You are what you eat!"

Also, to be able to live longer, we must take better care of ourselves. Wholeness is being complete, lacking nothing, and not broken or defective in any way. Women are taught to trash out what is not good for them, but replace it with a new good thing. It takes twenty – one days to learn how to replace an old habit with a new habit. Then, it takes a lifetime commitment to be diligent at maintaining it.

A mind is a terrible thing to waste, so nourish it daily with positive thoughts and feedback.

Growth – To come to be.
Mature – Fully developed, ripen, and characteristics of full development.

All girls will grow into adult women, but will they all grow maturely? We want women to become mature in all their ways. Ways such as their way of thinking, actions/reactions, and temperaments. Also, physically, emotionally, financially, and spiritually.

It all starts with what you eat.
Eat: To take in food; to consume or destroy.

Let's identify with what you are taking in, so we can know what you need to destroy.

To destroy is to ruin, demolish, raze, eradicate, and annihilate.

What do you eat for breakfast?

_____

_____

What do you eat for lunch?

_____

What do eat for dinner?

_____

Do you eat snacks? If so, what kind?

_____

What is your favorite meal?

_____

Why is it your favorite meal?

_____

When you eat your favorite meal, how much of it do you eat?

_____

How often do you eat it?

_____

Explain how you feel when you're eating it?

_____

Is your meal plan nourishing?

_____

Does it compliment who you are as an individual? If so, how?

_____

If you were to go out on a date, would he be surprised that you ordered that particular meal? Or would he say that fits you?

If it compliments who you are, he can pretty much surprise you with meals that will be satisfying to you.

Example:
A friend invited me out to dinner and he took me to a Thai restaurant. Though the gesture was nice and he was trying to invite me to try something new, he failed! If he had thought more about what complimented me, he would have taken me to a seafood, Italian, or soul food restaurant. He could have ordered anything off of the menu that I had never had, and it probably would have turned out great.

It's all about studying my patterns of what I eat.

As I said at the beginning of this chapter; you are what you eat.

What are you feeding your emotions?

_____

_____

_____

What does your mind feast off of on a daily basis?

_____

_____

What you are drinking is just as important as what you eat.

How often do you drink water?

_____

How many glasses do you drink a day?

_____

What about fruit juices?

_____

What about your alcohol intake?

_____

Let's discuss your fruit and vegetable intake.
Do you eat fruit and vegetables daily?

_____

What is your favorite fruit?

_____

What is your favorite vegetable?

_____

Have you ever tried fruit/vegetable smoothies?

_____

This is a great way of incorporating the nutrients you need in your daily intake.

Have you had a laxative lately?

_____

Please take a laxative and then start a new healthy regimen of better eating habits.
This is to detox your body, destroying anything that does not belong, and replacing it with what does belong.

Remember I am not a doctor and I do not know you personally, so before starting anything please consult your physician.

I shared in my book Women Overcoming Weight Loss how my son and I went from a plate to a saucer. We replace sodas with water, chocolate candy bars and chips with fruit and vegetables, and stopped eating after seven at night. As a result of changing my poor eating habits to rich healthy foods, I lost weight.

What I didn't share in that book was that I drank fruit smoothies three times a day as a meal replacement, during the summer, and lost an additional twenty five pounds.

Here are the ingredients:
- Five whole strawberries.
- Five cubed pineapples.
- One cup of raspberries and blueberries.
- Frozen Old Orchard Juice Pomegranate Cherry juice. ½ cup.
- 6ozs of yogurt of your choice.

- Rinse off fruit.
- Place ingredients into the blender.
- Blend and drink.
- Add ice if preferred.
- You can also add dry spinach, carrots, cucumbers, etc.

This is again just a suggestion to help you get the nutrients needed and help you lose weight physically.

We want to nourish our mind and body, so our soul will prosper.

3 John 1: 2
Dear friend, I am praying that all is well with you and that your body is as healthy as I know your soul is.

PHYSICAL THERAPY

Physical
Applicable to the body. To tangible matter as distinguished from the mental or spiritual.

Therapy:
A type of treatment.

Physical Therapy
The treatment of disease, injury, or deformity by physical methods such as massage, heat treatment, and exercise rather than by drugs or surgery.

Exercise
Is an activity designed to improve strength, endurance, something practiced to develop a skill.
To train; to make use of, as authority.

Some form of exercise is necessary to obtain and maintain strength and endurance, mentally, emotionally, and physically. We provide them with the essentials for all areas of their life. Movement keeps your body productive. This will develop a desire to look, feel, and be great!

Many people have medicated themselves with narcotics, prescription drugs, alcohol, and nicotine to treat a headache and/or heartache. But there are other methods, people can free their bodies from dis – ease. That can be simply getting a full body massage, along with heat treatment, to loosen the muscles and make your body less tense. Also, to simply stretch your muscles.

We are so tight and tensed from all the pressure, worrying, and overall discomfort. It's time to take ownership of our bodies again, and now!

We sacrifice our bodies for work, mates, children, and other people and things. Jumping out of bed, taking a quick shower, barely putting on lotion to moisturize our skin. We are doing good to put on deodorant, much less some perfume. This is only for a few of us. I know some of you won't walk to your mailbox without having on your face on (make-up) and your stilettoes.
We will bend over and touch our toes when enticing our man, to manipulate him to get what we want or to satisfy him. But we won't bend over on the side of our beds to pray, because we had such a long day. We refuse to bend over to exercise so we can be in better health and shape. The statement is not to degrade women, but to show women how we sacrifice our bodies. But we must start caring for our bodies.

Yes, I am talking to me as well. What's good for one, is good for all. We all fall short, but it's time for us to stand tall!

Do you remember the simple exercises we did in PE (physical education), in school? Yes, when we had to dress out in our shorts, t-shirts, and sneakers. Do you recall doing stretches before anything, warming our muscles? Then walking or running a lap or two to get our heart rate up. Jump n jacks, squats, sit-ups, and lunges.

My point is that it's time to go back to the simple things that meant a lot. These things brought on good change.

You may not be able to afford a trainer. That's fine; coach yourself. Go to the park and get on the swings, jump rope, or play hopscotch. Play tag with your children or race with them, by speed walking or running. You can ride a bike, skate, or hula-hoop.

Let's get moving!

Now for the married women, because you have a license to have sexual intercourse with your husband. Are you aware that sex is a form of exercise? Yes, ma'am it is! So stop being stingy and shutting down the garage because, it's a benefit.

I know you think I am contradicting myself from my previous statement, but I am not. So hear me out. We know that we are going to still help others, especially our family members, but we must learn to put our needs first and incorporate our needs when meeting others.

Let's add a little fun to physical.

So I explained how to have fun exercising with the kids. But to add a little more, you can play kickball, go skating, and play basketball. Do pretty much anything that gets you moving, so that you'll burn calories and begin to heal your body, physically, mentally, and emotionally.

Does any of this sound like fun yet?

Let's get Fysical! Yes, I know this will be fun for the married women.

Do you know you can bring fun exercises into your sex life? You can incorporate a couple exercises such as, squats, stretches (by touching your feet), woman push-ups, and sit-ups. I know you're saying that I am crazy! Not at all, but I realize we have creativity that lives within us that is trying to break through. But instead we keep it on lockdown, which has caused us to be so stiff, hard, and too strong in the wrong areas.

Everything that I've shared will cause you to laugh more and become flexible. Before you know it, the pounds will begin falling off right before your eyes.

Now do me a favor, look at that nice full body portrait that you placed at the front of the book. I need you to get a pen and circle everything you like about that beautiful figure. Then, take the pen and place an X on the parts that you want to change. I want you to begin inspecting your body and those areas you want to change. Begin loving on them. Yes, instead of hating your stomach, thighs, and arms; love them. If they are not as thin as they used to be, introduce them to physical therapy, which its nickname is EXERCISE!

It's time to get your WORKOUT on!

Here are some suggestions when starting a new workout regimen:

- Purchase a nice work out suit and walking/running shoes. Yes, please go and purchase you some vibrant colors and something light weight. The outfit will empower you, because we want to look good during the process.
- Make a commitment to the days and times that you will exercise regardless of what. You must be committed! Ex: I workout for thirty minutes on Mondays, Wednesdays, and Fridays.
- Choose a safe, well lit place, and make sure to bring bottle water. Always pay attention to your surroundings. I go to the park because I swing and use the bench to do arm lifts, sit-ups, and push-ups. If you choose outdoors, please have an alternative for the days when the weather is not in your favor.
- Inspect your surroundings. Find things you can use to help you meet your goal. Example: Stairs are my best friend. You can walk or run up and down the stairs.
- Choose a partner if you need that extra push. I chose not to have one, because when they fell off I did as well. So I've learned to motivate myself. Sometimes a partner can help or hinder you.
- Start off easy but finish strong! Whenever I fall off of my schedule and I have to start over again, I always start with light exercises. After that first week, I go hard.
- Rotate exercises, giving your body time to rest.
- Drink plenty of water afterwards. Always stay hydrated.
- I pray, praise, and worship while working out.

My prayer was that you would make it this far. I praise God that you have. I worship Him in Spirit and in Truth. I truly hope that this book has imparted something that was relevant to you being able to become all you need to be when you reach your destiny. Your destiny is to meet Jesus and hear Him say, "Job well done my good and faithful servant."

May His Love, Peace, Joy, Faith, Serenity, Patience, Perseverance, and Endurance be with you forevermore. May His Blessings and Miracles arrest you and hold you hostage until the day you meet Him again.

From one heart to another. Peace unto you.

NOTES

WOMENLATIONS!

You Did It!

You have successfully completed your one on one personal weight–loss inter-view. Acknowledging, accepting, and appreciating yourself for who you are, whose you are, where you are, and where you are going. You have been delivered and restored spiritually, mentally, emotionally, physically, socially, and soon financially. Congratulations!

Biblically the number seven means completion and the number eight means new beginnings. You have completed something to start something new. God bless your new season.

Remember every Christian has a past; and every sinner has a future. – Bishop Dale C. Bronner

I want to let you know there are two important things you must know. I encourage you to put this book up and never give it away. Why should I put it up? You will need it again. Why shouldn't I give it away? Because you will have to buy another one.

Weight loss is a process. You will gain weight and need to lose weight, so always keep this handy.

I am... I can... I will...

Blessings and miracles....

www.ingramcontent.com/pod-product-compliance
Lightning Source LLC
Chambersburg PA
CBHW081546040426
42448CB00015B/3237

9 780692 255384